I0844225

Mirrors of Alienation

The Self, The Other, and The Quest for Authentic Freedom

The Curious Philosopher

Copyright Page

© 2023 by The Curious Philosopher

All rights reserved. No part of this book may be reproduced in any form or by any electronic or mechanical means, including information storage and retrieval systems, without permission in writing from the publisher, except by a reviewer who may quote brief passages in a review.

This book is a work of non-fiction. Unless otherwise noted, the author and the publisher make no explicit guarantees as to the accuracy of the information contained in this book and will not be held responsible for any errors or omissions.

Published by Omniterra Media Inc

First Edition

Visit the author's website at www.curiousphilosopher.com

Disclaimer

The views and opinions expressed in this book are those of the author(s) and do not necessarily reflect the official policy or position of any other agency, organization, employer, or company. The contents of this book are for informational and educational purposes only and are not intended to serve as professional advice, diagnosis, or treatment.

The information provided in this book is believed to be accurate and reliable as of the date of publication. However, it may include some errors or inaccuracies, and no warranty or guarantee is provided regarding the accuracy, timeliness, or applicability of the content.

Readers are encouraged to consult with professional philosophers, educators, or other qualified professionals where appropriate for personalized advice. The author(s) and publisher shall not be liable for any loss, damage, or harm caused or alleged to be caused, directly or indirectly, by the information or ideas contained, suggested, or referenced in this book.

By reading this book, the reader acknowledges and agrees that they are solely responsible for how they interpret and apply the information contained herein.

This book may also include references to other works, studies, and sources. These references are provided for further reading and exploration and do not imply endorsement or validation of the specific theories, viewpoints, or interpretations presented in those works.

Chapter 1: Introduction

Once upon a time in the heart of France, amidst the hustle and bustle of Paris, a woman named Simone de Beauvoir embarked on a quest of thought that would forever change how we see ourselves and others. Born in a time when women were often sidelined, de Beauvoir wasn't one to be confined by society's expectations. Her mind was a vessel of curiosity, always sailing towards the horizons of understanding. Among her many explorations, one concept she delved into profoundly was the relationship between the 'Self' and the 'Other'. Now, these aren't complex philosophical terms, but simple words that hold a mirror to the essence of our social existence.

Imagine you're at a bustling party, full of laughter, chatter, and clinking glasses. You bump into someone, exchange smiles, and spark a conversation. In that brief interaction, two roles are at play. You are the 'Self' - the protagonist of your own story, viewing the world from your unique lens. Meanwhile, the person you just met is the 'Other' - someone distinct, with a narrative all their own. This interaction, as simple as it may seem, is a dance of perspectives where both individuals step into the shoes of the 'Self' and the 'Other'.

This dance is not always harmonious. Sometimes society plays a discordant tune, leading us to view the 'Other' through a lens of prejudice or fear. This lens distorts our understanding, forming a chasm between us and authentic connections. Simone de Beauvoir bravely peered into this chasm, seeking ways to bridge it. She believed that by recognizing and understanding our roles as both the 'Self' and the 'Other', we could find a path to authentic freedom—a state where we respect and understand each other's humanity, fostering a society ripe with empathy and equality.

Now, why should you or I, living in a world swirling with its own modern chaos, care about these ideas birthed in a Parisian café many decades ago? Well, because the ripples of 'Othering' continue to touch our shores. Whether it's the color of our skin, the accent in our speech, or the choice of whom we love, the dance of the 'Self' and the 'Other' continues, often with steps mired in misunderstanding.

This book aims to unravel the threads of de Beauvoir's insights, making them accessible to everyone—whether you're a seasoned philosopher or someone who's never dabbled in philosophy before. We'll journey through history, peek into the human psyche, and explore the societal structures that shape our interactions. Along the way, we'll gather keys to fostering a world where authentic freedom isn't just a lofty ideal, but a tangible goal.

As we delve into the chapters ahead, we'll dissect real-world examples of 'Othering', delve into the psyche of the 'Self' and the 'Other', and explore the roadmap towards authentic freedom as envisioned by de Beauvoir. We'll also examine how these age-old concepts resonate with our contemporary society, offering a lens to view, and perhaps, to change the world we live in.

So, let's step into the vibrant mind of Simone de Beauvoir, walk the tightrope between the 'Self' and the 'Other', and chase the horizon of authentic freedom. Through understanding, we embark on the first steps toward a society where the dance of the 'Self' and the 'Other' is one of harmony, respect, and mutual recognition.

Chapter 2: The Historical Construction of the "Other"

In the tapestry of human history, the threads of 'Self' and 'Other' have been woven with both delicate and harsh strokes, creating patterns of understanding and misunderstanding. To delve deeper into this, let's first understand what we mean by the 'Other'. It's a simple word, yet packed with layers of meaning. When we talk about the 'Other', we refer to someone or a group of people perceived as fundamentally different from ourselves. This perception of difference often paves the way for a divide, a line in the sand that separates 'us' from 'them'.

Now, let's hop onto a time machine and travel back to different eras to see how this notion of the 'Other' has played out. In ancient times, civilizations often regarded neighboring tribes or nations as the 'Other'. The Greeks, for instance, called non-Greeks 'barbarians', painting them as lesser beings. Fast forward to the era of explorations, and we see European explorers labeling indigenous people as savages, setting a stage for centuries of colonization and exploitation.

In more recent history, we've witnessed the harsh labels of 'Othering' being plastered across groups based on race, religion, or nationality. The grim shadows of the Holocaust, the heart-wrenching era of apartheid in South Africa, and the ongoing struggles against racial discrimination in many parts of the world are stark reminders of the 'Othering' narrative.

So, why does this 'Othering' happen? Often, it stems from a mix of fear, ignorance, or a thirst for power. By pushing someone into the box of the 'Other', a society, or a group within it, can establish a hierarchy – a pecking order that places some above others. This hierarchy seeps into the roots of social structures, often becoming a self-fulfilling prophecy. Those labeled as the 'Other' are treated differently, opportunities are snatched away, and a cycle of discrimination spins into motion.

But the tale doesn't end in despair. The story of the 'Other' is also a story of resistance and resilience. Through the ages, many have stood up against the tides of 'Othering', forging alliances, challenging norms, and striving for a world where the label of the 'Other' dissolves into a sea of shared humanity.

The impact of 'Othering' isn't just a social phenomenon; it's personal too. When we're stamped as the 'Other', it can mold our self-image, sometimes dimming the light of self-worth. Yet, it can also ignite a flame of rebellion and solidarity, leading to a quest for justice and equality.

As we explore the historical trails of the 'Other', we'll uncover not just the scars, but also the potential for healing and unity. The notion of the 'Other' isn't set in stone; it's a script that can be rewritten. By understanding the historical construction of the 'Other', we pave the way for a future where the 'Self' and the 'Other' can coexist, not in discord, but in harmony. Through the pages of history, we learn lessons of empathy, acceptance, and the boundless potential for change. And as we'll discover in the chapters ahead, the key to rewriting this script lies in recognizing our shared humanity, challenging the age-old narratives of 'Othering', and embracing the vibrant diversity that colors our world.

Chapter 3: De Beauvoir's Philosophical Landscape

In the garden of thought, Simone de Beauvoir planted seeds that sprouted into towering trees of existentialism and feminism. With a keen eye and a tender touch, she nurtured ideas that bloomed into discussions still vibrant in today's philosophical landscape. Her journey began with existentialism, a way of thinking that places our existence at the center stage, exploring the essence of our being, our freedoms, and the choices we make.

Now, let's add a sprinkle of feminism to this existentialist soil. Feminism, at its heart, seeks equality between genders, challenging the traditional roles and prejudices that have long kept women in the shadows. De Beauvoir blended these two flavors of thought, creating a rich stew of ideas that sought to understand the essence of our existence through the lens of gender.

Among the beautiful blossoms in de Beauvoir's garden is her seminal work, "The Second Sex". Picture this book as a bold flower, its petals unfurling to reveal the intricacies of how society perceives women as the 'Other'. In her exploration, de Beauvoir delves into the many ways in which women have been relegated to a secondary status, seen through a distorted lens of preconceived notions rather than as individuals with their own essence and ambitions.

"The Second Sex" isn't just a critique; it's a call to action. It urges us to shatter the shackles of traditional gender roles, to look beyond the veil of the 'Other', and to see the individual standing there – with dreams, desires, and a unique essence.

Now, let's venture beyond the bounds of de Beauvoir's garden and explore the philosophical forest where her ideas cross-pollinate with those of other thinkers. Her discussions on the 'Other' echo the ideas of her contemporaries and those who came before her. The branches of her thought entwine with those of philosophers like Jean-Paul Sartre and Friedrich Nietzsche, creating a rich canopy of discussion around identity, freedom, and our place in the social tapestry.

Yet, de Beauvoir's voice rings distinct amidst this chorus of philosophical musings. Her focus on the gendered experience of 'Othering' adds a unique hue to the existentialist and feminist discussions, painting a picture that's as complex as it is captivating.

As we wander through de Beauvoir's philosophical landscape, we'll find a path that leads us to a vantage point. From here, we can glimpse the vast expanse of ideas stretching across the horizon, each one a stepping stone towards understanding the dance between the 'Self' and the 'Other'. With each chapter, we delve deeper, not just into de Beauvoir's mind, but into the heart of our shared human experience. Through her lens, we begin to see the world anew, inviting us to challenge, to question, and to strive towards a society where the 'Other' is no longer a shadow, but a reflection of our shared humanity.

Chapter 4: The Dual Role: Being the "Self" and the "Other"

Imagine you are at a bustling marketplace. The aroma of fresh produce fills the air, and the clamor of bargain-hungry shoppers rings through the crowd. As you maneuver through the aisles, you bump into an old friend. You exchange pleasantries, reminisce about old times, and promise to catch up soon. In this simple encounter, you played the role of the 'Self,' the protagonist in your narrative, while your friend was the 'Other' in your world. Yet, for your friend, they were the 'Self' and you were the 'Other'. This is the dual role we play in the theatre of life - a dynamic that Simone de Beauvoir delved deeply into.

Now, let's break down this dual role a bit. In any social interaction, we are both subjects and objects. As subjects, we act, we decide, we experience. But simultaneously, we are objects in the eyes of others, perceived and interpreted through their lenses. This dual role isn't a rigid costume we put on; it's a fluid identity that shape-shifts with every interaction.

Now, what does this mean for us, psychologically and socially? On a personal level, this dual role can affect our self-esteem, our confidence, and our sense of identity. If we are constantly seen as the 'Other', it might sow seeds of doubt or feelings of exclusion. Yet, it can also foster a sense of uniqueness, a pride in our individuality.

On a broader social canvas, this dual role colors the fabric of our interactions. It's the brushstroke that defines the 'us' versus 'them' narrative, creating ripples across communities and societies. The dynamics between the 'Self' and the 'Other' can either build bridges of understanding or walls of prejudice.

Let's delve into some real-world scenarios to understand this better. Picture a classroom, a microcosm of society. Here, the dual role plays out in myriad ways. A student from a different cultural background might be seen as the 'Other' by his peers. Yet, this 'Otherness' could be a source of richness, bringing a fresh perspective to discussions.

In the workplace, the dance between the 'Self' and the 'Other' continues. A woman in a male-dominated field might struggle with the label of the 'Other'. Yet, her unique experiences can contribute to a more diverse and inclusive environment.

In neighborhoods, this dual role shapes the sense of community. The family next door with a different lifestyle might be seen as the 'Other'. Yet, engaging with them, understanding their worldview, can lead to enriching interactions and a broader understanding of the world.

Through these scenarios, we begin to see the potential for both discord and harmony in the dynamics between the 'Self' and the 'Other'. It's a delicate dance, but with every step, there's an opportunity to challenge preconceptions, to break down barriers, and to create a rhythm of understanding and acceptance.

As we journey through the chapters ahead, we'll continue to explore the depths of this dual role. We'll delve into the paths leading towards authentic freedom, and the ways in which understanding the dance between the 'Self' and the 'Other' can lead us towards a more inclusive, empathetic, and harmonious society. Through the lens of Simone de Beauvoir, we'll continue to unravel the complex, yet beautiful, tapestry of human interactions, each thread a story, each color a step towards understanding the 'Self,' the 'Other,' and the world we share.

Chapter 5: The Path to Authentic Freedom

In the heart of Paris, amidst the whispers of budding leaves and the soft rustle of the Seine, Simone de Beauvoir sowed a seed of thought that germinated into the concept of authentic freedom. But what is this authentic freedom she spoke of? Well, it's about embracing the essence of our existence, appreciating the dance between being the 'Self' and the 'Other', and fostering a world where respect, understanding, and empathy flourish.

Now, how do we stride down the path towards this lofty ideal? The first step is a gaze inward, recognizing our dual role in the social ballet. We are both the dancer and the audience, the 'Self' and the 'Other'. This recognition isn't a solitary endeavor but a collective awakening. It's about seeing and being seen, understanding and being understood.

Yet, this path isn't strewn with roses; it has its share of thorns. Recognizing our position as both the 'Self' and the 'Other' can be a daunting task. It requires peeling layers of preconceptions, facing the mirrors of truth, and often, challenging the norms that have long defined societal structures.

Now, let's envision a world where we've embarked on this journey towards authentic freedom. Imagine a community where individuals appreciate the richness of diverse experiences, where the 'Other' is no longer a distant entity, but a fellow traveler on the path of understanding. This isn't just a poetic vision but a pragmatic aspiration. Authentic freedom has the potential to reshape our personal and societal relationships profoundly.

On a personal level, it's about forming connections that are rooted in respect and understanding rather than prejudice. It's about experiencing the joy of discovering the world through myriad lenses, each interaction a step towards broader horizons of understanding.

On a societal canvas, authentic freedom paints a picture of inclusivity, equality, and mutual respect. It's about crafting policies that acknowledge the dignity of every individual, fostering environments that celebrate diversity rather than shun it.

Let's delve into some discussions around this. Imagine a school where the curriculum is designed not just to fill minds with facts but to open hearts to the beauty of diverse experiences. Imagine workplaces where the ladder of opportunity is accessible to all, irrespective of gender, race, or background. Imagine neighborhoods where the doors of dialogue are always open, where the 'Other' is welcomed with a smile of understanding rather than a frown of prejudice.

Through the kaleidoscope of Simone de Beauvoir's insights, we see that authentic freedom isn't a distant dream but a tangible goal. It's a journey of a thousand steps, each step a move towards a world where the 'Self' and the 'Other' dance to a rhythm of respect, empathy, and understanding.

As we venture through the pages ahead, we'll continue to explore the nuances of this journey. We'll examine the roadblocks, celebrate the milestones, and envision the beautiful vistas that authentic freedom can unveil. Through the lens of de Beauvoir's philosophical insight, we'll continue to navigate the complex yet captivating landscape of human interactions, each step a stride towards a world where authentic freedom is the melody that orchestrates the dance between the 'Self' and the 'Other'.

Chapter 6: Contemporary Relevance and Applications

As we navigate through the bustling streets of today's world, the whispers of Simone de Beauvoir echo through time, their resonance felt amidst the skyscrapers of modern thought and the crowded avenues of social interaction. The notions of the 'Self' and the 'Other' are not relics of the past; they are living, breathing dynamics playing out in the here and now. Let's embark on a journey to explore the modern-day manifestations of "Othering" and the ripple effects they create across the social fabric.

In today's global village, the shades of 'Othering' are as diverse as the human palette. They emerge in the exclusion of immigrants, in the discrimination against people of different races, religions, or sexual orientations. The headlines often tell tales of division, of walls built out of fear or ignorance. Yet, amid these narratives, there's a growing awareness, a stirring of consciousness that beckons us towards a more inclusive perspective, much in line with de Beauvoir's vision of authentic freedom.

Now, how are de Beauvoir's ideas faring amidst the currents of today's sociopolitical landscape? Her concepts continue to inspire debates, fuel movements, and provide a framework for understanding the dynamics of identity and freedom. The fight for gender equality, the movements against racial discrimination, and the advocacy for LGBTQ rights are arenas where her ideas find a loud echo. They challenge us to look beyond the superficial labels, to appreciate the essence of every individual, and to strive for a society free from the shackles of prejudice.

Let's zoom into some real-world scenarios to see how the pursuit of authentic freedom is unfolding. Take the #MeToo movement, for instance. It's a clarion call against the entrenched norms that have long perpetuated gender-based discrimination and violence. It's a movement that resonates with de Beauvoir's call for recognizing and challenging the dynamics of the 'Self' and the 'Other'.

Across the globe, individuals and communities are also stepping up to rewrite the narrative of 'Othering'. In the heart of war-torn regions, there are individuals extending hands of friendship across historical divides, defying the labels of the 'Self' and the 'Other'.

Through these case studies, we see glimpses of authentic freedom breaking through the clouds of prejudice. These are not just isolated instances but parts of a larger narrative of change, a testament to the enduring relevance of de Beauvoir's ideas.

As we navigate through the complex terrain of contemporary society, the compass of de Beauvoir's philosophy provides a direction towards a more inclusive, empathetic, and just world. It's not a smooth sail, but a voyage filled with storms and calm, challenges, and opportunities.

Through the looking glass of the present, de Beauvoir's ideas are not mere philosophical musings, but catalysts for action, lenses through which we can envision and work towards a world that celebrates the richness of human experience, transcending the bounds of the 'Self' and the 'Other'.

As we turn the pages of this chapter and delve into the ones ahead, we continue to unravel the tapestry of human interactions, each thread a narrative, each color a step towards a world where authentic freedom isn't just a philosophical concept, but a lived reality.

Chapter 7: Critiques and Counterarguments

In the world of ideas, every theory, every concept, has its day in court. And so does the philosophy of Simone de Beauvoir. Her notions about the 'Self', the 'Other', and the path to authentic freedom have been met with both applause and critique. This chapter takes you on a guided tour through some of these debates, offering a balanced view of the criticisms and counterarguments surrounding de Beauvoir's ideas.

Now, let's delve into some of the criticisms aimed at de Beauvoir's philosophy. Some critics argue that her ideas might oversimplify the complex dynamics of human interactions. They say the world is not just a stage with the 'Self' and the 'Other' playing roles, but a multifaceted arena where numerous factors shape our perceptions and behaviors.

Others have pointed out that de Beauvoir's notions may seem too idealistic in a world rife with deep-seated prejudices and systemic barriers. They wonder if the path to authentic freedom she envisioned is too steep to tread in reality.

Now, on the flip side of the coin, supporters of de Beauvoir have crafted counterarguments. They argue that her philosophy doesn't seek to oversimplify, but to illuminate the core dynamics of human interaction. They point out that by understanding the dance between the 'Self' and the 'Other', we are better equipped to navigate the complex social terrain.

Regarding the criticism of idealism, proponents say that de Beauvoir's vision is not a utopian dream but a beacon of aspiration. They argue that her ideas serve as a compass, guiding individuals and societies towards more equitable and empathetic interactions.

Now, let's delve a bit into the limitations and the enduring relevance of de Beauvoir's concepts. Every theory has its boundaries, and de Beauvoir's philosophy is no exception. It may not provide a one-size-fits-all solution to the myriad challenges of human society. Yet, its core message holds a timeless appeal. The quest for authentic freedom, the understanding of the 'Self' and the 'Other', remains as relevant today as it was in the streets of Paris where de Beauvoir pondered over the human condition.

In a world where the echoes of 'Othering' reverberate across continents, her ideas invite us to pause, reflect, and engage in a dialogue that transcends the superficial divides. They urge us to embark on a journey of self-discovery and societal reflection, to challenge the status quo, and to foster a world where the essence of every individual is recognized and celebrated.

As we explore the critiques and counterarguments, we are not merely engaging in an academic exercise, but embarking on a voyage that sails through the turbulent waters of debate towards the calm shores of understanding. Through this voyage, we glean insights that sharpen our understanding of de Beauvoir's philosophy, appreciating its nuances, its strengths, and its areas of growth.

So, as we close this chapter and look ahead, we carry with us a richer, more nuanced understanding of the philosophy of Simone de Beauvoir. We are better equipped to engage with the world, to challenge our preconceptions, and to contribute to the ongoing dialogue that shapes the course of human thought and action. Through the lens of critique and counterargument, we continue our exploration of the landscape of ideas, each step a stride towards a deeper understanding of the human experience.

Chapter 8: Conclusion

As we find ourselves at the closing pages of this exploration, let's take a moment to look back at the landscape we traversed together. Our journey began at the heart of Simone de Beauvoir's musings, where the concepts of the 'Self' and the 'Other' were introduced. Through her lens, we explored how these ideas have shaped, and continue to shape, the dynamics of personal and societal relationships.

We ventured through history, observing the manifestation of 'Othering' across different eras and societies. Our expedition led us to the core of de Beauvoir's philosophical landscape, where existentialism and feminism intertwined to offer a unique perspective on human interactions. We explored the dual role we all play as the 'Self' and the 'Other', delving into the psychological and social implications of this dynamic.

Our narrative unfolded onto the path of authentic freedom, a quest to transcend the superficial labels and to embrace a deeper understanding of our shared humanity. We examined the contemporary relevance of de Beauvoir's ideas, witnessing how they resonate in today's sociopolitical landscape. And we navigated through the critiques and counterarguments, enriching our understanding of de Beauvoir's philosophical contributions.

Now, as we stand at the crossroads of reflection and action, the essence of this exploration beckons you to continue the journey. It invites you to engage in self-reflection, to examine your perceptions, your interactions, and your place in the social tapestry. It urges you to participate in societal analysis, to challenge the norms, to question the status quo, and to contribute to the discourse that shapes our collective destiny.

The quest for authentic freedom isn't a destination but a continuous journey. It's about fostering a culture of empathy, understanding, and mutual respect. It's about recognizing the humanity in the 'Self' and the 'Other', transcending the superficial divides, and weaving a social fabric rich with the colors of diversity and the threads of inclusivity.

The thoughts of Simone de Beauvoir serve not as a final answer, but as a compass guiding us towards a horizon where the 'Self' and the 'Other' dance in harmony, where authentic freedom is the melody that orchestrates the rhythm of human interactions.

As you turn the pages of your own narrative, may the essence of this exploration resonate in your thoughts, in your interactions, and in your quest for a deeper understanding of the human experience. The dialogue doesn't end with the last word of this book; it continues with every question you ask, every perspective you consider, and every step you take towards a world where the dance between the 'Self' and the 'Other' is a celebration of our shared humanity.

About The Curious Philosopher

Welcome to The Curious Philosopher, your dedicated platform for diving deep into the world of philosophy. We are more than just a YouTube channel or a book publisher. We are a beacon of enlightenment, making complex philosophical concepts accessible and engaging for all.

Our YouTube channel is a rich repository of philosophy made simple. We take the profound and often complex ideas from the world of philosophy and break them down into digestible, easy-to-understand content. From the ancient wisdom of Socrates to the existentialist thoughts of Sartre, we cover a broad spectrum of philosophical schools and thoughts, making philosophy accessible to everyone, regardless of their background or prior knowledge.

As a book publisher, we take the same approach, transforming intricate philosophical theories into comprehensible narratives. Our books are not just collections of words, but vessels of wisdom that make philosophy approachable and relatable. We believe that philosophy should not be confined to academic circles, but should be available to all who seek to understand the world and their place in it.

At The Curious Philosopher, we believe in the power of curiosity and the pursuit of knowledge. We are here to stoke the fires of your curiosity, to guide you on your intellectual journey, and to help you navigate the fascinating world of philosophy.

If you are someone who is not afraid to question, to explore, and to learn, then you are in the right place. Join us on this journey of exploration, as we make philosophy easy to understand, one concept at a time.

Be sure to visit our Youtube channel at:

https://www.curiousphilosopher.com/youtube

You can also visit us on the web at

https://www.curiousphilosopher.com

Welcome to The Curious Philosopher. Stay curious. Stay enlightened.

www.ingramcontent.com/pod-product-compliance
Lightning Source LLC
Chambersburg PA
CBHW060911260726
48661CB00008B/3578